JUST ONE OF THOSE THINGS

Wick Poetry Chapbook Series Three
Maggie Anderson, Editor

Any Kind of Excuse
Nin Andrews

Orphics
Leonard Kress

Just One of Those Things
Sarah Perrier

The Several World
Will Toedtman

JUST ONE OF THOSE THINGS

Sarah Perrier

The Kent State University Press
Kent & London

Library of Congress Catalog Card Number 2002067523
ISBN 0-87338-759-7
Manufactured in the United States of America

06 05 04 03   5 4 3 2 1

The Wick Poetry Chapbook Series is sponsored by the Stan and Tom Wick
Poetry Program and the Department of English at Kent State University.

Library of Congress Cataloging-in-Publication Data
Perrier, Sarah, 1973–
      Just one of those things / Sarah Perrier.
            p.   cm.—(Wick poetry chapbook ; ser. 3, no. 3)
      ISBN 0-87338-759-7 (alk paper) ∞
      I. Title.   II. Wick poetry chapbook ; ser. 3, no. 3

PS3616.E77 J87 2003
811'.6—dc21   2002067523

British Library Cataloging-in-Publication data are available.

So goodbye dear, amen.
Here's hoping we'll meet now and then.
It was great fun
but it was just one of those things.
    —Cole Porter

CONTENTS

ACKNOWLEDGMENTS

Grateful acknowledgment is made to the publications in which these poems, sometimes in slightly different versions, first appeared. *Cimarron Review:* "Ass," "Meeting You: A Definitive Plan," and "Porch with No Swing"; *The Cream City Review:* "How to Be Eight" and "Patience"; *The GSU Review:* "Notes on First Kisses"; *The Ledge:* "How Not to Sleep Around"; *Phoebe:* "Fresh"; *River Oak Review:* "Translation."

MEETING YOU: A DEFINITIVE PLAN

I will not buy two goldfish and name them both Elizabeth Taylor
because there is no telling them apart. I will not decide
they are both Scorpios simply because I am, and because I think
they are mysterious for their distracted way of pouting
around their bowl, turning the curves smoother
each time. Their wet world will not tip like a steaming teapot
into a cup. No cat will lap up its tragic good fortune.
You will not sell me two new fish at a dollar apiece
plus ten more for a new bowl to replace the one gravity got
and you will not miscalculate the sales tax and I will not
not get my change back. Chances are, you will not even work
at Bud's Sea and Sky Shop. So in case that's you shopping
the family planning aisle out of wedlock, don't
let our white-haired family pharmacist
with the spooky, wall-eyed stare catch me smirking
as he assures the woman (who I pray is not your girlfriend)
all the merchandise is "fresh." And since you probably aren't
her supportive older brother checking the date on every box
of every brand don't think to think about some grand plan
passing you by. Tonight I am as simple as the world's last love poem:
I pay for multivitamins, I shoplift a pack of Freshen-Up.
I leave the door swinging behind me, right in front of you.

PORCH WITH NO SWING

—after Edward Hopper's Summer Evening

Her clothes are more bare
than the light and I am sure
the young man is glad.
Late, on a porch with no swing
his request seems more daring.

Her clothes are more bare
than the light. Her red-headed
frown squares out her jaw.
Curtains hang inside the door;
she still hasn't caught his drift.

Her clothes are more bare
than the light. Only I think
he's wearing her shoes.
Heavy curtains do not catch
in the breezeless summer air.

Her clothes are more bare
than the light. Her red-headed
frown squares out her jaw.
Curtains hang inside the door;
he still hasn't caught her drift.

HOW TO BE EIGHT

Imagine that you and your dog are in the front yard.
The dog must be wet, and possibly has soap still sudsing his fur
because you're eight and, even though I'm telling you how to
do this, you're going to get part of it wrong. *Good. Very good.*

Feel the sharp small slap of the dog's wet tail against your thigh.
Accidentally spill half the bucket of water you're carrying
on yourself. Miss the dog entirely with the other half of the water.
Now wait briefly, as if you are trying to figure out what to do next.

You are trying to be helpful—and that's good—but now you must
stop helping for a moment. Your dog is shaking himself off. His head
and body seem to twist in opposite directions at the same time.
Now your dog is tossing himself in the grass, sending loose blades

into the air. His tail and paws fly upwards like a seizure.
You would like to try this, I know. You have watched your parents
practice this at night in their bed. Go ahead, you're eight
and you are eager to grow up. Notice how damp the lawn is.

Remember to make soft snuffling sounds. Wait for your mother.
(Think how she must be about a million years old in dog years.) Wait
for her to bang the door open by throwing her hip against the latch
while kicking the sticking spot loose. She never spills a drop

of her drink. Get up from the grass and tell her you are sorry.
Actually *be sorry* at this point. As sorry as you were last night,
awakened by strange sounds then slapped for being a snoop.
Consider this the growing list of your own shortcomings.

NOTES ON FIRST KISSES

Allen Wexler thought he was the first, and I let him
strut that fact for days. The only myth of first kisses

is that there is only one. The first kiss on the lips,
the first one with tongues. The first with feeling

(it's probably fear). How can you believe
a word I say, once you know where my mouth

has been? Josh Elias asked first. Kenny Hudgins
should have brushed his teeth better. Can you

believe a word I say, until you know what else
my mouth can do? Shut up and kiss me, fool.

ON THE PRINCIPLE OF PAIRING IN NATURE

Don't look in the obvious places.

Friends with good intentions will tell you to employ simple principles of logic: If you want to hunt big game, they will say, you must find it where it lives. Want a lion? Get thee to the dark continent of love where prides of doctors and lawyers run free through happy hours, night clubs, and upscale retail centers. If you point out that you could be a gazelle they will repeat their advice, as if it's you who didn't get the point.

But maybe you are looking for the arty type. Order pizza, they say. The musician willing to starve for his art delivers. The painter delivers. The sculptor, performance artist, struggling first novelist, aspiring actor/director, documentary filmmaker, and songwriter all deliver. Call. Wait. He will come to you fresh, hot and in thirty minutes or less. He will come guaranteed.

If you are too hungry to wait that long, go to the drive-thru. Look at the speaker and be sure to speak directly to it. There is a chance you will hear a promise of love so rich you'll devour it, want more. You'll want to drive through again and again, circling the parking lot just to hear the voice promise he'll "bewitch you in a moment."

Take classes at the community center, they say. Even the ones that don't interest you. Yogacize. Learn to look in every crowd for someone dressed like your soul mate. Always look alert and receptive. Dress like someone else's soul mate. Most of all, don't look like you're looking. But don't look and—*poof!*—you disappear.

ASS

Sure, my ex tells me, *you can say "ass"*
with anything. For emphasis especially.

Like the word is the white blouse my mother said went
with everything. The black patent leather

shoes that dress up any outfit, but don't really
reflect up. It just doesn't seem like a compliment

to say a woman has a "fun ass sense of humor."
The conversation is going nowhere, but thank God

it's midsummer so I can play like I swallowed a gnat
because it's believable and I'd rather let my ex

(we're still friendly) feel sorry for me about that.
Let him think I flinched over some bug

he couldn't even see, so he can slap my back squarely
and try to hand me my drink again, the ice cubes

squeaking against the curve of the tumbler as they melt
into the already wet air. *So the dog won't listen*

he'd cheer at me if he figured out the tiny fly was a fake
and I'd hear him out, so he wouldn't have to feel

the daily impotence of people who make their livings
watching people cry. Let him think what he likes.

What he likes is the woman in his office
who always wears a black bra and has a tattoo

(A teddy bear on the inside of her wrist!
It's no bigger than a dime! he gushed).

I think the bug trick might be working.
My ex just says *those candles never work,*

do they? and rattles the loose ice in his glass. Citronella
burns through the neighborhood. The dog returns

to its post, a mat of plastic grass near the door,
and snouts around suspiciously. Animal possessiveness

(we're still friendly) uncocks its ears,
braces for this evening's mosquitoed assault.

ACADEMIC AFFAIRS

Why don't you love me, and we can hit the road together,
cruise the lecture circuit and tell other single people

about the work it takes to make it work. Together,
we'll talk talk talk about the necessity of long-term

memory and the value of the grudge. Your flipchart
of my body parceled out like a butcher's map

shows the exact locations of too much and too little
with tiny stuck-on arrows, their sharp points as fine

as my revenge: reading poems instead of lectures,
each one a reminder of other men I left for doing less.

Afterward, alone again, come up beside me, nuzzle my ear
and quote Foucault: *Tomorrow, sex will be good again.*

Now add *But tonight you're on your own.* This is how
itinerant scholars of loss communicate: quote, footnote.

Our end notes and marginalia are full of longing for the pet
projects we can't let go, yours on fixing up my life, mine

a love poem I've been working on for years. It reads,
I can take it if you can; I can take it if you can.

It didn't much matter anymore if he was a bullfighter, a cattle roper, or a rodeo clown. You wanted to feel callused hands, watch them run smooth along the fence rails. His palms would almost shine, daring the wood to splinter.

In Clear Spring there's nothing but a field full of trucks and the Clear Spring Saloon, but you were still singing about the Terlingua—not thinking of Waylon or Willie, but mainly, of the boys. I told you to buckle up.

But *Sweet God* how you saw them! Rowdy, cocksure, and lovely in their swaggers. You'd kiss them hard just to prove their lips could bruise. In Seguin someone asked us what two girls from way up North were doing in Texas. You said you were down here looking for the whole enchilada.

Rodeo isn't the same thing as *The Rodeo* and neither of us knew that leaving Chicago. Not cows, *cattle,* they told us. Half way out of Austin we stopped counting tumbleweeds and cows. When I asked for directions to The Rodeo at a gas station in Luchenback they told me *It's in February.*

PATIENCE

First the sound of metal rolled flat
by open places, and then the press
of the whistle muscling through
brambles. The sound of darkness
hunting itself in the backyard

like a streak of pure weight.
On the other side of the tracks
someone fiddles with a radio.
Someone taps one fingernail
on the steering wheel or stands

in a doorway, ready to wish
in case a caboose comes by. Suppose
just once, there weren't coal cars
but loads of cut diamonds blaring
their fire straight down

the limits line between this world
and the next. Or better still,
a passenger train to bring
the one face you've been waiting for,
with its slightly rumpled brow

and delicate wrists. That skin that asks
to be touched because inch
by inch it is becoming an expanse. Now
say *hello* or *I have always loved this weather*
or *I have always loved you.*

HOW NOT TO SLEEP AROUND

Cats call out their crazy love
and the amphitheater alley bellows back
their late-night heat. The creekbed
cuts corners, and its scratched shale banks scrape and creak
like furniture. Familiar sheets twist against your own
unmixed sweat. In the other world, lovers carry on
and someone clutches you like a handbag
in a bad part of town. Someone hollers

keep it down! and summer settles in
while you name each of its sounds, name the heat
itself, as it comes in cycles and waves you on
toward that one last thing you're waiting
to feel: either cooler nights and quiet sleep,
or a hotter way to cool your heels.

WATER SPEAKS TO OUR SUBCONSCIOUS SELVES

The power was out, so the t.v. wouldn't work and the garage door was stuck shut. Everyone stayed in. No moths' wings opened or closed in the darkness above the front door. *Tip: Drink half a glass of water before bed. Remembering your dreams is as easy as drinking the other half when you wake up.*

I couldn't tell if anyone ever stepped out on anyone else. All along, when other parents were running around, I figured mine were busy doing something different. I mean, I guessed they must have been. I went to bed early. A whole lake froze and its shale cliffs eroded.

Trouble was they never said how big a glass. And by morning, you'd think they'd have come back on, the lights. I was so thirsty my voice cracked for good. I still can't remember if they were in color, what I looked like, or if I could fly.

ARTIFICIAL ATTACHMENTS

No one wants to rush into anything anymore, at least
that's how the story goes when we meet. We've all
been hurt by someone, we're moving slow this time,
sure it's better to be lonely and cautious than foolish

and lonely all the same. Now the rush to retreat
has become so fashionable I can't order coffee
without the cashier telling me how the change he gives
"doesn't mean anything." So careful, we crawl

through the city, scouting locations for the perfect date
and the perfect breakup, the best first kiss and the last
forced goodbye. So when I stop you on the street and whisper
kiss me, it's not your mouth I want, but the memory

of being kissed just there, and impulsively. I have planned
each detail down to the day of the week and the weather,
fattening fantasy with a hint of intent. But I get impatient
waiting for some invisible hand to move you; won't you

move faster—come over here and take my hand
in front of the amputated sign for RTIFICIAL LIMBS—
I've written you in according to plan. We'll kiss;
by the next line you'll love me; three later I'll leave.

TRANSLATION

—a lament for Emperor Wu of the Han and his concubine

Suppose it was her meatloaf he loved
and that they had made plans to buy her a color t.v.
as soon as they could. Suppose he loved her

unreasonably, with the feverish intensity of a sailor
who's been out to sea too long. That in their kisses
this woman could hold her hand around the thick knot

of his braid and he could finally be brave enough
to whisper something into her ear that might never be
whispered back. Suppose in his grief he could be angry

and smoke cigarettes in an American diner.
Set the table with a cup of black coffee,
and a newspaper open to the crossword puzzle

and let him cry it on out, because the waitress
in a pink, frilled uniform has hands he remembers
stretching their slim fingers out toward him

from square palms. Let her be the one to ask:
does he know what he wants? He wants clocks
not to run clockwise, and not at the slow secondhand's pace.

CARNIVALESQUE

Bargains were struck. Firemen dressed as clowns, Jaycees' Wives made snow cones, and the Chamber of Commerce sold raffle tickets. Andrea Nelson wore perfume and stole a hanky from her father's drawer.

We were learning Brad Higgins kissed with one eye open and Jeff Meyers wouldn't kiss a girl until she touched his cock. In the lost and found, a thin gold band—the confirmation ring Julia Jennings gave some boy. Mothers wept. Fathers blinked. The brass band clanged away.

Then the ferris wheel came down and the fun house folded up—it turned out to be a trailer home—painted, gutted, and rewired. The whole town buzzed and blared. Blame had to be misplaced: Some sentences began "My daughter. . . ." Some began "Those carnies."

FRESH

I.

When Kevin Miller's mother called me *fresh*
before swaying up her driveway I didn't know
her New Jersey twang was from New Jersey

or that when she called me
fresh she meant to make me
sorrier than her son was for the game

he started with kisses. I ran after him
until his wrist was fast in my grip
and his belly was flat in the dirt. The soft

pop of his skin beneath my teeth
is still as fresh as the sting in my mouth
where I stretched it sore at the corners.

His mother stopped in her tracks when I spat
the missing bit of his dirty cotton shirt at her heels
and she spat back with *fresh*. Suppose his response

had been that sharp. Suppose my kneecaps
hadn't cracked two of his twiggy ribs
and left him forgetting how to handle

his next breath. Suppose he had been
heels-dug-in stubborn and refused to run.
The messages our bodies send us

and deliver us from—quick as currents
running to ground—snap and arc
under the force of our telling (the synapse

filters flash and the story is recast):
If he hadn't run away, he could have won.
And now if the knot of his scar could untie itself

and slip back into skin, it would only be
one more thing he left behind
when I watched his mother load half

a houseful of her, her wisdom
and her furniture, onto a truck
and head back to New Jersey.

II.

Before he began, the dentist shook
his thumb over his right shoulder, asked me
if I "wanted one like that." Kevin Miller

was long gone, and my trophy—my chipped
incisor was filed smooth. By summer, I learned
to throw out a hip and to carry a comb.

I hung out at the corner of Rollerskate
and Ten Speed with a pack of cigarettes
I knew how to light but couldn't yet

smoke. On the corner
we played "Truth" and let
the good lies slide until Nicole

Ryan dared Steve Swisher to a game,
then fired off a pack of lies.
Had she, or would she ever? *Yeah.*

With a boy? *Yeah.* With Brian
Wilburne? *We were gonna but
he just had his braces tightened.*

With a girl? *No way, Steve.
You're the only queer I know.*
And none of us said a word.

Then Megan, who knew about sins
of omission, heard her mother call, and Ruth,
who always played by the rules, said it was hers.

Then Ben and Adam Morgan rode off
without a word. Nicole spat out her gum,
said *Let's don't tell, right? We don't*

ever tell. When he asked me if I wanted
one like that, I wondered if the dentist meant the girl
or her thousand dollar smile.

Did I really have to choose? Could I
tell him anything without a word
like *complicit?*

III.

We still don't tell. None of us would ever
say a word about how Nicole
was easier than a boy, or mention

how she let us kiss her, so long
as we kept our eyes open
and did what she told us to do:

No. The boy puts his hands here.
The trouble with secrets is keeping them
quiet enough. Is choosing who

to tell each story to. Nicole never told
anyone who didn't already know and I
never told anyone at all. I lied to Allen

Wexler through my straightened teeth;
said it just came natural, because maybe it did
for someone. In the woods, behind the traffic rails

at the dead-ends of streets; in basements
and bedrooms and borrowed cars;
in the alley behind the drugstore

and under the bleachers at away games,
the difference between postulate
and theorem was made manifest

on a familiar scale, without a reminder
that failures have always been
part of the proof. The exclusive properties

of either *saving myself* or *giving it out*
on the cheap seemed less exclusive
the night Rob McKerney kicked me out

of his car for not wanting to go all the way.
He had said we would just *practice,* but Rob
didn't want to practice like Nicole and I had.

I hadn't considered not believing him
when he said we wouldn't do it in his car.
Whichever way, the story is the same.

IV.

I can only allow for so much discretion
and if my stories seem to hedge their bets,
it's a habit I've picked up with experience:

John Ackerman pulled my hand to his crotch
during an assembly. What if I had
pulled away instead of trying

to imitate what I told Rob McKerney I wouldn't do?
Then John Ackerman wouldn't have held
his books low as he left the auditorium

and I wouldn't have wondered what John
Ackerman's mother said when she found
those jeans in the wash. Then I wouldn't

have said yes when Theresa Vincente
asked *That's it? That's all it is?*
She expected stories of hands

under my shirt and voices dropping
to soft guttural gasps. Not the simple
synchronous looks away. Not quiet

disavowals and throat-clearings without even,
simply, a thank you. The whole truth
is invariably only part of the story—the skin

over the flesh and bone of experience.
I have let what comes first hand
come first. Everything else resists

translation into narrative—the story doesn't end.
There is no moment I can point to, say
This is when things changed. Kevin Miller,

I'd still pin you down in the dirt,
if only to tell your mother to take back
the time she called me fresh; if only

to ask Nicole Ryan if what happened
happened only to me. If only to say
none of this happened only to my body.

PERSONAL POEM

Be my material! SWF/MFA seeks solution to invention problem. Me: young poet (red/br) well-versed, strong interest in voice. Some cross-genre tendencies. You: scary uncle meets muse. You: literate, but ill-tempered. You: Fickle. You have some major hangups. You is not me. You breaks my heart. I goes on from there.